Dedicated to:

*My family who taught me
antecedence of morality*

Nurturing Hair

Indian Medicinal Plants Used In Hair Care

Dr. Bhagyashali Karle

M.Sc., Ph.D., SET

About the Author

Dr. Bhagyashali Karle, M.Sc., Ph.D., SET. Assistant Professor, Department of Botany New Arts, Commerce and Science College, Ahmednagar. She has completed her graduation and post-graduation in Botany from Savitribai Phule Pune University, India. She has qualified SET (State Eligibility Test) and Ph.D. on medicinal plants from Savitribai Phule Pune University, India. She has extensive research and teaching experience at various levels in academics. Her area of research interest is antioxidant activity of plants, taxonomy and ethnobotany.

Preface

Indiscrete effect of growing interest in herbal cosmetics of the world and Indian conventional hair care practices encouraged me to focus on the topic. It is a great privilege to publish my first book, Nurturing Hair: Indian Medicinal Plant Used in Hair Care. As this is a sensible and intimate topic for humans in all the eras, the book covers the overview of traditional hair care plants in India. It is an honest attempt to cover the most used hair care plants with their taxonomy, uses and images of the plants. A book provides brief information of particular traditional uses of plants for common hair problems and active constituents present in it. This book will motivate to the researchers and students for further cosmeceutical study, as active constituents of the plants are important for various types of preparations. The review has done by market and literature survey. The material included in this book has taken from various sources like research journals, articles, books floras and websites. Extensive bibliography is provided at the end of the book. I declare that, the material obtain from the other sources has been acknowledged. Valuable suggestions from the readers will help me to improve the book.

bhagyashali 4444@rediffmail.com

Bhagyashali Karle

Acknowledgement

I express my gratitude to the Hon. Management of Ahmednagar Jilha Maratha Vidya Prasarak Samaj, Ahmednagar for support. I would like to acknowledge Dr. B. H. Zaware, Principal, New Arts, Commerce and Science College, Ahmednagar for consisting support. I would like to express my thanks to Dr. C. S. Arsule, Head of Department of Botany, for his guaidance. I am very thankful to Dr. J. R. Mulay mam for a great idea about work. Special thanks to Dr. A. A. Adsul for plant identification and photographic help. I am thankful to Ayurved Vyaspetth, Ahmednagar and MPKV, Rahuri for allowing photography in their Dhanvantari gardens. I am eternally grateful to Prof. V. S. Kale sir and Prof. B. M. Gaykar sir for their right direction always. Thanks to my family who promote to grow always, without them book never have been completed. Thanks to my supportive friends Monika, Manisha Sunita, Shivani for being with me. Finally, my gratitude and thanks to all, who directly and indirectly assisted me to publish the book.

CONTENTS:

Preface

Acknowledgement

List of the plants

List of the plants:

1. *Abrus precatorius* Linn.

2. *Acacia concinna* (Willd.) DC.

3. *Acacia arabica* (Lam.) Willd.

4. *Acorus calamus* L.

5. *Achyranthes aspera* L.

6. *Aegle marmelos* (L.) Corr.

7. *Aloe vera* (L.) Burm.f

8. *Allium cepa* L.

9. *Allium sativum* L

10. *Annona squamosa* Linn.

11. *Azadirachta indica* A. Juss.

12. *Bacopa monnieri* (Linn.) Wettst.

13. *Brassica compestris* L.

14. *Butea frondosa* Roxb.

15. *Calotropis gigantea*(L.) Dryand.

16. *Celastrus paniculatus* Willd.

17. *Centella asiatica* (L.) Urb.

18. *Cicer arietinum* L.

19. *Citrus limon* (L.) Burm. f.

20. *Clitoria ternatea* L.

21. Cocos *nucifera* L.

22. *Cyperus scariosus* R.Br.

23. *Datura stramonium* L.

24. *Eclipta alba* (L.) Hassk

25. *Emblica officinalis* Gaertn.

26. *Eucalyptus globulus* Labill.

27. *Glycerrhiza glabra* L.

28. *Hedychium spicatum* Sm.

29. *Hibiscu srosa-sinensis* L.

30. *Indigofera tinctoria* L.

31. *Jasminum officinale* L.

32. *Lawsonia inermis* L.

33. *Linum usitatsimum* L.

34. *Mentha piperita* L.

35. *Murraya koenigii* (L.) Spreng.

36. *Nardostachys jatamansi* (D.Don.) DC.

37. *Prunus dulcis* (Mill.) D.A.Webb

38. *Psoralea cordata* (Thunb.) Salter

39. *Ricinus communis L.*

40. *Rosa damscena* Mill.

41. *Rubia cordifolia* L.

42. *Sapindus trifoliatus* L.

43. *Sesamum indicum* L.

44. *Tagetus erecta* L.

45. *Terminalia belarica* (Gaertn.) Roxb.

46. *Terminalia chebula* Retz.

47. *Trigonella foenum-graecum* Linn.

48. *Withania somnifera* (L.) Dunal

49. *Ziziphus mauritiana* Lamk.

50. *Zingiber officinale* Roscoe.

.

INTRODUCTION

Confidence breeds beauty- Estee lauder

The concept of beauty and cosmetics is just as primordial as mankind and civilization. Especially women are always obsessed with beauty and have the notion that beauty is completes with healthy, beautiful hair. Hence they have been using natural things to enhance their own beauty since ancient times. Even nowadays people in rural areas using plants as a traditional cosmetic because those are easily accessible, cheap and without side effects. The science that improves appearance, is cosmetology, a very popular branch of science and ayurvedic cosmetics. It has been practicing since Indus Valley Civilization. India is rich in biodiversity especially in spices and medicinal plants, several herbs are used in ayurvedic hair cosmetics products and that worked. Herbal cosmetics not only beautifying the hair but also helps to protect against any external effects. It enriches the body with nutrients and many useful minerals. Those herbs are secret about healthy and attractive Indian hair as 'Indians have the world's best hair' (The Hindu, Chennai, July 09, 2010).

Common hair problems around the globe are hair splitting, frizzing, drying, premature graying, falling, alopecia, thinning and dullness of hair and increasing because of modern lifestyle. Hair oil Shampoo, conditioner, serum, dye, spray are some hair products for maintenance of the hair. Those products are more effective if exercise, healthy diet, sufficient sleep and a pleasant mind is in support. Hair has great value in our appearance so, many plants-based cosmetics are being popular.

cosmetics and home remedies. Herbal Cosmetics have great demand in the global market and it is a valuable gift of nature and we should thankful for that. Some plants have significant value to overcome that daily hair problem, without purification even can apply in crude form.

In present study botanical name and common names of plants are listed with their family and distribution. Habit of the plant, Plant part used, uses and active constituent present in the plants also noted by the literature survey. Active constituent of the plant will be key point for future work. Those plants almost easily available all over India; and popular for a long time for hair care. Present study will provide the platform to further research in hair cosmetics, as plant name in Marathi, Hindi and Sanskrit is given

So, this book may useful to all beautiful people around, as plants don't know boundaries....

Materials and Methods

In this review of Indian medicinal plants, plants which have hair care potentials are summarized by a market survey in Ahmednagar city, to know the plants used in different hair cosmetics products. List of plants was confirmed by Ayurvedic Pharmacopoeia of India (1999) and Book of Indian Medicinal Plants by Kirtikar and Basu (1995) [5, 56]. In current study fifty medicinal plants listed from different angiosperm families. For the correct and latest scientific name, distribution and habit selected authentic sites such as https://indiabiodiversity.org/,www.tropicos.org,http://www.theplantlist.org, [129,135,134,] were visited. Regional floras such as flora of Presidency of Bombay (1903), Flora of British India (1875), Flora of Marathwada 9198) [22, 43, 72] were also referred.

Vernacular name of the plants given in Marathi, Hindi and Sanskrit with the help of authentic sites such as https://www.indianmedicinalplants,

http://www.biodiversityofindia.org

[126,131].Photography was done in different places of Ahmednagar including Dhanwantari Udyan Rahuri, Dhanwantari Udyan Ahmednagar by Sony cybershot 2.0 camera. For some rare plants, photographic help was taken by other source [136]. Active constituent of plants reviewed by literature survey with the help of research papers, articles, books and cites.

Enumeration

The plants enumerated in alphabetical order of botanical names followed by family, vernacular names (Marathi, Hindi and Sanskrit), habit, distribution, plant part used, uses and active constituents found in it.

1.

Botanical Name: *Abrus precatorius* Linn.

Family: Fabaceae

Vernacular Names (Marathi, Hindi & Sanskrit): Gunja, Rati, Gujja.

Habit: A perennial wiry, twining climber.

Distribution: Throughout India.

Plant Part Used: Seed

Uses: Paste of seed is used for hair wash; promote hair growth [99, 112].

Active Constituent: Abrin A and B, triterpenoid, saponins, abraline, abrasine, abricin, abrusgenic acid [99].

2.

Botanical Name: *Acacia Arabica* (Lam.) Willd.

Family: Mimosaceae

Vernacular Names (Marathi, Hindi & Sanskrit): Babhul, Babul, Barbura.

Habit: Spiny tree

Distribution: At all drier parts of India

Plant Part Used: Pods

Uses: It is used to remove dandruff and helps in increasing the hair length [38].

Active Constituent: D-galactose, L-arabinose, arabic acid, oxidase, peroxidase [127].

3.

Botanical Name: *Acacia coccinea* (Willd.) DC.

Family: Fabaceae

Vernacular Names (Marathi, Hindi & Sanskrit): Shikekai, Shikakai, Saptala.

Habit: Shrub

Distribution: Tropical forest of India.

Plant Part Used: Seeds

Uses: It is used for washing hair. Promote hair growth, prevent dandruff & gives the shining of hair [87].

Active Constituent: Vit. C, nicotine, oxalic acid, citric acid, succinic and tartaric acids [117].

4.

Botanical Name: *Acorus calamus* L.

Family: Acoraeae

Vernacular Names (Marathi, Hindi & Sanskrit): Wekhand, Vacha, Vachha.

Habit: A semiaquatic perennial aromatic herb with creeping rhizomes and tuberous roots.

Distribution: Grow in marshy places; plentiful in Kashmir, Manipur and Naga hills.

Plant Part Used: Dried rhizome.

Uses: It strengthens the hair roots, prevents hair loss and gives the shine of hair. It also controls dandruff [24].

Active Constituent: Eugenol [24].

5.

Botanical Name: *Achyranthes aspera* L.

Family: Amaranthaceae

Vernacular Names (Marathi, Hindi & Sanskrit): Aghada, Aghara, Apmarga.

Habit: An erect or procumbent annual or perennial herb with the woody base.

Distribution: Throughout India, Common weed along the roadside, undergrowth along forest borders during the rainy season.

Plant Part Used: Root

Uses: It cures dandruff and keeps healthy hair [107].

Active Constituent: Oleanolic acid, B-sistosterol [57,67].

6.

Botanical Name: *Aegle marmelos* **(L.) Corr.**

Family: Rutaceae

Vernacular Names (Marathi, Hindi & Sanskrit): Bel, Bel, Adhararuha.

Habit: A middle sized slender aromatic armed tree.

Distribution: Wild in Central and Southern India, cultivated all over India.

Plant Part Used: Seed

Uses: Fruit pulp is used as a substitute as a shampoo and removes dandruff [80].

Active Constituent: d-limonene, citronellal, citral, pcyrnene, cumin, cineol [78].

7.

Botanical Name: *Alliumcepa* **L.**

Family: Liliaceae

Vernacular Names (Marathi, Hindi & Sanskrit): Kanda, Pyaj, Sukandak.

Habit: A hard perennial sub-erect with bulbs.

Distribution: Cultivated in India.

Plant Part Used: Bulb

Uses: It prevents dandruff and hair loss. It also shines hair prevents and kills lice. [97,68,80].

Active Constituent: Vit. C and E, sulfur-containing compoundallicine [97].

8

Botanical Name: *Allium sativum* L.

Family: Liliaceae

Vernacular Names (Marathi, Hindi & Sanskrit): Lasoon, Lahsoon, Lahsoona.

Habit: A hard perennial sub-erect with bulbs made up of cloves.

Distribution: Cultivated in India.

Plant Part Used: Bulb

Uses: For the treatment of scalp acne, alopecia (patchy baldness), kills lice, prevents hair loss [80,6].

Active Constituent: Alliin, an oxygenated sulfur amino acid [6].

9.

Botanical Name: *Aloe vera* (L.) Burm.f

Family: Liliaceae

Vernacular Names (Marathi, Hindi & Sanskrit): Korphad, Kumari, Dhrutkumaree.

Habit: Succulent herb with bulbs.

Distribution: Planted in Indian gardens, found in a semi-wild state in many parts of the India.

Plant Part Used: Pulp of the succulent leaves

Uses: Stimulate the growth of hair; prevent hair fall and dandruff. It also helps to combat dry and brittle hair [11,64].

Active Constituent: Vit. A, C and E, campesterol, β-sisosterol, barbaloin,Salicylic acid [83,114,49].

10.

Botanical Name: *Annona squamosa* Linn.

Family: Annonaceae

Vernacular Names (Marathi, Hindi & Sanskrit): Sitaphal, Sharifa, Krishna beeja.

Habit: A large evergreen, straggling shrub or small tree.

Distribution: A commonly cultivated tree in the garden, sometimes found wild also.

Plant Part Used: Dried seeds

Uses: Seed paste used to kill lice, prevent dandruff and hair fall. It inhibits scalp inflammation [112,125].

Active Constituent: Vit. C and A, iron, anonaine, annonacin, squamocin [125].

11.

Botanical Name: *Azadirachta indica* A. Juss.

Family: Meliaceae

Vernacular Names (Marathi, Hindi & Sanskrit): Kadunimb, Neem, Nimbaka.

Habit: A large evergreen tree.

Distribution: Wild in the forest of Maharashtra, often planted all over India.

Plant Part Used: Fruit, leaf, bark, seed.

Uses: Used for dandruff and killing lice, prevent hair loss [41,43,44].

Active Constituent: Nimbosterol, nimbolin bark. Seed oil has azadiradione, azadirone, meliantriol and meldenin. Leaves contain nimbolide, quercetin and B-sitosterol [40].

12.

Botanical Name: *Bacopa monnieri* (Linn.) Wettst.

Family: Scrophulariaceae

Vernacular Names (Marathi, Hindi & Sanskrit): Brahmi, Bhramhi, Neerbrahmi

Habit: A small creeping, glabrous or succulent annual herb.

Distribution: Throughout India in wet, damp and marshy areas.

Plant Part Used: Stem and leaf

Uses: Promote hair growth; it also removes dandruff and lice [127].

Active Constituent: Brahmine; herpestine. betulic acid, d-mannitol, stigmasterol, β-sitosterol [40].

13.

Botanical Name: *Brassica juncea* (L.) Czern.

Family: Brassicaceae

Vernacular Names (Marathi, Hindi & Sanskrit): Mohari, Sarso, Saraso

Habit: Annual herb

Distribution: Throughout India.

Plant Part Used: Seed

Uses: Seed oil used as a hair tonic for growth also blackens hair, antidandruff [104, 51].

Active Constituent: Seed contains Vit. B complex, A and E sinigrin, gluconapin, sinapine [104].

14.

Botanical Name: *Butea monosperma* (Lam.) Taub.

Family: Fabaceae

Vernacular Names (Marathi, Hindi & Sanskrit): Palas, Palash, Kinsuka.

Habit: A deciduous tree.

Distribution: Common throughout India.

Plant Part Used: Leaf and Resin.

Uses: Hair growth and removes dandruff [92].

Active constituent: Leaf has palmitic and lignoceric, glucoside, Kino-oil containing oleic and linoleic acid. Resin has allophanic acid, Z- Amyrin, e-sitosterone, jalaric esters and laccijalaric esters [92].

15.

Botanical Name: *Calotropis gigantean* (L.) Dryand. Family: **Asclepiadaceae**

Vernacular Names (Marathi, Hindi & Sanskrit): Rui, Aak, Bhanu.

Habit: A small tree.

Distribution: Common throughout India.

Plant Part Used: Latex

Uses: Remove dandruff and prevent hair loss [16].

Active constituent: It contains β-amyrin, giganteol, giganteol, α and β calotropeol, and isogiganteol [47].

16.

Botanical Name: *Celastrus paniculatus* Willd.

Family: Celastraceae

Vernacular Names (Marathi, Hindi & Sanskrit): Kangunii, Malkanguni, Jyotishmati.

Habit: An unarmed large perennial deciduous climbing or scrambling shrub.

Distribution: Found in tropical and subtropical Himalayas.

Plant Part Used: Fruit and seed

Uses: Remedy for against dandruff and hair graying. It enhances the hair growth make hair silky [123,46,84].

Active constituent: Acetic, benzoic, formic, linoleic, linolenic, palmatic and stearic acids. Celapagine, celapanine, celastrol, celastrine, malkanguniol and alkangunin [18].

17.

Botanical Name: *Centella asiatica* (L.) Urb.

Family: Apiaceae

Vernacular Names (Marathi, Hindi & Sanskrit): Ekapani, Ballari, Mandukaparni.

Habit: A prostrate perennial faintly aromatic creeping herb, rooting at the nodes.

Distribution: Common in moist grounds and along the sides of cultivated fields.

Plant Part Used: Whole plant

Uses: Tonic and stimulant for hair growth, hair conditioning, conditioning. Promote healthy scalp condition and prevent hair loss [31].

Active constituent: Fresh leaves contain a glucoside asiaticoside and asiatic acid vellarine, pectic acid and resin present in roots and leaves [118,40].

18.

Botanical Name: *Cicer arietinum* L.

Family: Fabaceae

Vernacular Names (Marathi, Hindi & Sanskrit): Harbara, Chana, Jivana.

Habit: Much-branched annual herb.

Distribution: Largely cultivated pulse crop in most parts of India.

Plant Part Used: Seed and leaf

Uses: It is used to treat hair fall, premature greying and dandruff [89].

Active constituent: Vit. A, B, and C. It also has carotenoids, aredaidzein, formononetin, secoisolariciresinol, genistein, matairesinol and biochanin [128].

19.

Botanical Name: *Citrus limon* (L.) Burm. f.

Family: Rutaceae

Vernacular Names (Marathi, Hindi & Sanskrit): Limbu, Nimbu, Nimbuka.

Habit: Shrub

Distribution: Cultivated all over India.

Plant Part Used: Peelandjuice

Uses: It is used to control oil output in hair, gives a special gloss to the hair. It prevents dandruff, hair loss and works as a pH modifier [80,115].

Active constituent: Vit. C, limonene, calcium, Pectin, citric acid, malic acid, citrain, terpineol, camhenium and fellander [90].

20.

Botanical Name: *Clitoria ternatea* L.

Family: Fabaceae

Vernacular Names (Marathi, Hindi & Sanskrit): Gokaran, Aparijita, Girikarnika.

Habit: A pretty perennial twinner with blue or white flowers.

Distribution: A common garden plant; also occur among hedges all over India.

Plant Part Used: Flower

Uses: Hair growth promoter and gray hair recover, strengthen hair follecle [130].

Active constituent: Flavonol glycoside, myricetin, quercetin and anthocyanins [3].

21.

Botanical Name: *Cocos nucifera* L.

Family: Arecaceae

Vernacular Names (Marathi, Hindi & Sanskrit): Naral, Nariyal, Kalpvriksha.

Habit: A tall palm

Distribution: Cultivated in the hot damp regions of India especially near the sea.

Plant Part Used: Fruit

Uses: Kernel oil is well-established oil, used as base hair oils and tonics. It protects the hair from protein loss, conditioning and gives thicken hair and pleasing luster [96,54,22,93].

Active constituent: Oleic and linoleic acids as triglycerides. Tocopherols, tocotrienols, phytosterols, trimyristin, tristearin, trilaurin, tripalmitin andlauric acid [32,36].

22.

Botanical Name: *Cyperus scariosus* R.Br.

Family: Cyperaceae

Vernacular Names (Marathi, Hindi & Sanskrit): Lawala, Nagarmotha, Chakranksha.

Habit: Delicate slender sedge has deep brown tubers.

Distribution: Throughout India.

Plant Part Used: Tuber/ Rhizome.

Uses: Rhizomes are used for washing hair, stimulates sebaceous glands near hair roots. Hair strengthening and scalp rejuvenating properties [15].

Active constituent: Sesquiterpenes- cyperone, selinene, sugeonol, kobusone, cyperene, cyperotundone, pinine, patchulenone, and isokobusone [110].

23.

Botanical Name: *Datura stramonium* L.

Family: Solanaceae

Vernacular Names (Marathi, Hindi & Sanskrit): Dhotra, Dhatura, Dhattura.

Habit: A glabrous or farinose annual herb

Distribution: Cultivated in India, often found wild.

Plant Part Used: Fruit

Uses: Juice applied to the scalp to prevent hair fall and dandruff [109,103].

Active constituent: The major constituent is atropine, hyoscamine and scopolamine [45].

24.

Botanical Name: *Eclipta alba* (L.) Hassk

Family: Asteraceae

Vernacular Names (Marathi, Hindi & Sanskrit): Maka, Bhringraj, Bhringraj

Habit: An erect or prostrate annual succulent herb.

Distribution: Common weed in moist situations throughout India.

Plant Part Used: Leaf

Uses: To remove dandruff and fungal infection. It promotes hair growth and the blackening of hair [94,111].

Active constituent: It contains wedololactone, ecalbasaponins ß-amyrin, ecliptine, desmethyl-wedelolactone, hentriacontanol, stigmasterol, heptacosanol, [69,108].

25.

Botanical Name: *Emblica officinalis* Gaertn.

Family: Euphorbiaceae

Vernacular Names (Marathi, Hindi & Sanskrit): Awala, Amla, Amalaki.

Habit: A small or medium sized deciduous tree.

Distribution: Common in mixed deciduous forests of India, often cultivated in home gardens.

Plant Part Used: Fruit and seed

Uses: Amla provides nutrition to hair and also causes darkening of hair. It promotes hair growth and improves retention [24,74].

Active constituent: Rich in Vit. C and mineral; phosphorus, iron and calcium. It has mucrosin, trigalloyglucose, olio-palmitoarachidin, ellagic acid, phyllenbic acid, phyllantidine and phyllantine [19,].

26.

Botanical Name: *Eucalyptus globulus* Labill.

Family: Myrtaceae

Vernacular Names (Marathi, Hindi & Sanskrit): Nilgiri, Safeda, Haritparni

Habit: Tree

Distribution: All over India.

Plant Part Used: Leaf

Uses: It promotes hair growth and reduces dandruff [31].

Active constituent: Cineole and volatile aldehyde as well as terpenes, alcohol and phenol [40].

27.

Botanical Name: *Glycyrrhiza glabra* L.

Family: Fabaceae

Vernacular Names (Marathi, Hindi & Sanskrit): Jeshthamadh, Mulethi, Jalyashti.

Habit: A hardy sub-erect perennial herb or undershrub.

Distribution: Cultivated in Jammu Kashmir, Punjab and Sub-Himalayan tracts.

Plant Part Used: Root

Uses: The root is good for improving hair growth; it keeps the scalp moist, hydrated and help strengthen the hair shaft [26].

Active constituent: Liquorices, glycyrrhizin, steroids, β-glycyrrhetinic acid [20].

28.

Botanical Name: *Hedychium spicatum* Sm.

Family: Zingiberaceae

Vernacular Names (Marathi, Hindi & Sanskrit): Kapurkachari, Sandharlika, Gandhmulika

Habit: A perennial rhizomatous herb or a tall tree with rootstock

Distribution: Found in Himalayas subtropical forest

Plant Part Used: Rhizome

Uses: It is used in hair oil especially to prevent baldness and hair fall; it also prevents dandruff [86].

Active constituent: It contains pentadecane and an aromatic ester (ethyl p-methoxycinnmate) [86].

29.

Botanical Name: *Hibiscus rosa-sinensis* L.

Family: Malvaceae

Vernacular Names (Marathi, Hindi & Sanskrit): Jaswand, Gudhal, Ajagandhika.

Habit: An evergreen woody, glabrous showy shrub.

Distribution: Grown as an ornamental plant in gardens throughout India.

Plant Part Used: Flower

Uses: Used to stimulate hair growth and prevents premature graying of hair. It used to control dandruff [1,53,105].

Active constituent: Anthocyanins, flavonoids, citronellol, geranoil, linalool, camphene, eugenol and pienene [39,40].

30.

Botanical Name: *Indigofera tinctoria* L.

Family: Fabaceae

Vernacular Names (Marathi, Hindi & Sanskrit):
Neel, Neeli, Rangpushpi.

Habit: It may be an annual, biennial or perennial depending on the climate in which it is grown.

Distribution: Found in tropical and temperate India.

Plant Part Used: Leaf

Uses: It helps in control itching and regaining hair its color. Prevent premature falling, thinning and early graying of hair [4].

Active constituent: Indigotine, indiruben, rotenoids [101].

31.

Botanical Name: *Jasminum officinale* L.

Family: Oleaceae

Vernacular Names (Marathi, Hindi & Sanskrit):
Jai, Chameli, Mallika.

Habit: A large scrambling or twining shrub.

Distribution: Native of Northwest Himalayas, wildly grown throughout India.

Plant Part Used: Flower, leaf

Uses: As perfume in oil [95].

Active constituent: Jasminol, Jasminolactone, multiforin, olueropin, benzyl benzoate, farnesol, nerolidol, eugenol, linalool, indole and jasmine [98].

32.

Botanical Name: *Lawsonia inermis* L.

Family: Lythraceae

Vernacular Names (Marathi, Hindi & Sanskrit): Mehandi, Henna, Mendhika.

Habit: A glabrous, much branched shrub or small tree.

Distribution: Cultivated and naturalized all over India.

Plant Part Used: Leaf

Uses: Used for hair dyeing, promotes hair growth, cools the scalp, treat dandruff, makes hair shiny. Prevent hair loss and balancing the pH of the scalp [61,121].

Active constituent: Lawsone (2-hydroxyl-1, 4 nepathaquinone) is the chief constituents of the plant as a coloring matter. Hennatannin, lacoumarin, lawsonin and lawsonic acid [104].

33.

Botanical Name: *Linum usitatsimum* L.

Family: Linaceae

Vernacular Names (Marathi, Hindi & Sanskrit): Jawas, Alsi, Atashi.

Habit: Herb

Distribution: Cultivated throughout India

Plant Part Used: Seed

Uses: Promote hair growth, gives shine to hair and prevent hair fall, used to treat alopecia [14].

Active constituent: Oleic and linolenic acid (Omega3), Palmitic acid and stearic acid [81].

34.

Botanical Name: *Mentha piperita* L.

Family: Lamiaceae

Vernacular Names (Marathi, Hindi & Sanskrit): Pudina, Podina, Rochani

Habit: A small annual herb.

Distribution: Cultivated all over India

Plant Part Used: Leaf

Uses: Helps to get rid of stubborn dandruff and accelerates hair growth [75].

Active constituent: Octanol, limonene, β-Caryophyllene, menthofuran, menthone, menthol, pulegone, menthyl acetate, cineole, *trans*-sabinene hydrate and neomenthol [27].

35.

Botanical Name: *Murraya koenigii* (L.) Spreng.

Family: Rutaceae

Vernacular Names (Marathi, Hindi & Sanskrit): Kadhipatta, Karipatta, Girilimb.

Habit: A medium sized tree.

Distribution: Native of Eastern Ghats. Found all over India on the banks of rivers and streams.

Plant Part Used: Leaf

Uses: It prevents hair graying work as hair tonic [112].

Active constituent: It contains nicotinic acid, sterols amino acids, and flavonoids, also contains Vit. A, B, C, and E [132].

36.

Botanical Name: *Nardostachys jatamansi* (D.Don.) DC.

Family: Valerianaceae

Vernacular Names (Marathi, Hindi & Sanskrit): Balchuda, Balchari,Jatamasi

Distribution: Grown widely in India.

Plant Part Used: Rhizome

Uses: oil promotes the growth of hair and imparts blackness [23,51].

Active constituent: It contains resin, volatile oil, jatamansic acid and ketones (Jatamansone and nardostachone) [23,85].

37.

Botanical Name: *Prunus dulcis* (Mill.) D.A.Webb

Family: Rosaceae

Vernacular Names (Marathi, Hindi & Sanskrit): Badam, Badam, Badama.

Habit: A middle sized tree

Distribution: In cooler parts of Punjab and Kashmir.

Plant Part Used: Seed

Uses: It nourishes hair and helps to soften and strengthens it, reduces premature hair fall. Stimulate hair growth [77,79,11]. **Active constituent:** Pruansin, decosterin, sitosterol, iacin, ascorbic acid, biotin, thiamine, riboflavin, folic acid and tocopherols [11,35].

38.

Botanical Name: *Psoralea cordata* (Thunb.) Salter

Family: Fabaceae

Vernacular Names (Marathi, Hindi & Sanskrit): Bawachi, Bukchi, Somraji.

Habit: An erect annual herb

Distribution: Found on roadsides and waste places throughout India.

Plant Part Used: Seed

Uses: It is used to improve the color, prevent hair loss [55].

Active constituent: Angelicin, bakuchiol, limonene, γ-elemene, β-caryophylenoxide, α-elemene, 4-terpineol, linalool, geranylacetate [55].

39.

Botanical Name: *Ricinus communis L.*

Family: Euphorbiaceae

Vernacular Names (Marathi, Hindi & Sanskrit): Earandi, Earand, Amanda.

Habit: An erect woody perennial shrub.

Distribution: Cultivated all over India.

Plant Part Used: Seed

Uses: Seed oil used to darkening hair and prevent hair fall, irradiate dandruff [68,60].

Active constituent: Ricin, ricinoleic acid and ricinine [65].

40.

Botanical Name: *Rosa damscena* Herrm.

Family: Rosaceae

Vernacular Names (Marathi, Hindi & Sanskrit): Gulab, gulab, Vruttpushpa.

Habit: An erect woody perennial shrub.

Distribution: Cultivated all over India.

Plant Part Used: Flower

Uses: Hair growth and shine. It also controls excess oil [133].

Active constituent: β-citronellol, nonadecane, geraniol, and nerol and kaempferol [17].

41.

Botanical Name: *Rubia cordifolia* L.

Family: Rubiaceae

Vernacular Names (Marathi, Hindi & Sanskrit): Manjistha, Manjit, Manjisthha

Habit: A very variable prickly creeper or climber.

Distribution: Throughout India and hilly districts of Konkan.

Plant Part Used: Rootandstem

Uses: It is effective in preventing hair loss, used as hair dye [29].

Active constituent: Coloring matter obtains from purpurin and munjistin. Xanthopurpurin, pseudopurpurin, mollugin and alizarin [29].

42.

Botanical Name: *Sapindu strifoliatus* L.

Family: Sapindaceae

Vernacular Names (Marathi, Hindi & Sanskrit): Ritha, Ritha, Rishtak

Habit: A medium sized to a large deciduous tree or shrub.

Distribution: Commonly cultivated in villages of South India and West Bengal.

Plant Part Used: Fruit

Uses: Fruit coat extract used as hair cleanser [68].

Active constituent: Saponins, sapindoside A and B, oleic and stearic acid. Vit. A, D, E, K [8,28,117].

43.

Botanical Name: *Sesamum indicum* L.

Family: Pedaliaceae

Vernacular Names (Marathi, Hindi & Sanskrit): Til, Teel, Tilmin.

Habit: An erect branched or unbranched annual herb.

Distribution: Cultivated all over India.

Plant Part Used: Seed

Uses: Seed oil cures hair loss and nourishes the dry scalp, reduces the damaging effects of sunlight and pollution. It helps strengthen hair shafts and roots, darken hair [60,73,120].

Active constituent: Seeds are fairly rich in thiamine and niacin, sesamin [63].

44.

Botanical Name: *Tagetus erecta* L.

Family: Asteraceae

Vernacular Names (Marathi, Hindi & Sanskrit): Zendu, Genda, Sandu

Habit: Hairy erect annual herb.

Distribution: Cultivated throughout India.

Plant Part Used: Flower

Uses: Used as a hair dye [76].

Active constituent: Ocimenes, limonene, terpinene, myrcene, tagetone, dihydrotagetone, tagetenone, β-ocimene, β-caryophyllene and eugenol [9].

45.

Botanical Name: *Terminalia bellirica* (Gaertn.) Roxb.

Family: Combrataceae

Vernacular Names (Marathi, Hindi & Sanskrit): Behada, Behara, Bhootvasa.

Habit: A large deciduous tree.

Distribution: Found in the plains and lower hills, throughout the forest of India.

Plant Part Used: Fruit

Uses: Seeds extract used for hair dyeing preparation [30].

Active constituent: Thannilignan, arjungenin, belleric acid, bellericoside, gallic acid, ellagic acid and ß-sitosterol [58].

46.

Botanical Name: *Terminalia chebula* Retz.

Family: Combretaceae

Vernacular Names (Marathi, Hindi & Sanskrit): Hirda, Harra, Jivpriya.

Habit: A moderate sized or large deciduous tree.

Distribution: Abundant in Northern India, the forest of Bihar, West Bengal and Maharashtra especially in Konkan.

Plant Part Used: Fruit

Uses: It reduces hair greying, used as a hair tonic, hair dye [50, 34].

Active constituent: Chebulic acid, chebulinic acid, gallic acid, ellagic acid, punicalagin, and tannic acid. Flavonoids- quercetin, catechin and kaempfer [52, 59].

47.

Botanical Name: *Trigonella foenum-graecum* Linn.

Family: Fabaceae

Vernacular Names (Marathi, Hindi & Sanskrit): Methi, Methi, Bahuparni

Habit: An aromatic erect, annual herb.

Distribution: Cultivated in many parts of India.

Plant Part Used: Leaf and seed.

Uses: Seed extract is used as a hair cleanser, cools the scalp and strengthen the root hair. It helps to control dandruff and premature hair fall [119, 82].

Active constituent: Diosgenin, trigonelloside gitogenin and tigogenin, from leaves. Vitexin and isovitexin from seeds [12, 13].

48.

Botanical Name: *Withania somnifera* (L.) Dunal

Family: Solanaceae

Vernacular Names (Marathi, Hindi & Sanskrit): Ashwagandha

Habit: An erect evergreen tomentose shrub.

Distribution: Throughout the drier region of India

Plant Part Used: Flower

Uses: The plant is good for the circulation of the scalp, improving the structure of the hair. It is also used against greasy hair, dandruff and enhances melanin production [106, 66].

Active constituent: Roots contain withanolides, withaferin A, isopellertierine, anferine, somniferine, tropine, cuscohygrine, choline, anaferine, sitoindoside and steroidal [10, 48].

49.

Botanical Name: *Zingiber officinale* Roscoe.

Family: Zingiberaceae

Vernacular Names (Marathi, Hindi & Sanskrit): Aale, Adarak, Nagara

Habit: An erect herb with the rhizome.

Distribution: Widely cultivated in India.

Plant Part Used: Rhizome

Uses: Helps in hair loss treatment makes hair stronger, shiny and healthy. It stimulates hair growth, treating scalp [116,124,91].

Active constituent: Oleoresin, gingerol, shogaol, zingerone and paradol. Potassium, magnesium, and vitamins [100,116].

50.

Botanical Name: *Ziziphus mauritiana* Lam.

Family: Rhamnaceae

Vernacular Names (Marathi, Hindi & Sanskrit): Bor, Ber, Badarah.

Habit: A small tree or large shrub is usually armed.

Distribution: Common in hotter parts of India, cultivated in gardens or found in wild also.

Plant Part Used: Leaf

Uses: Leaves are used for hair wash [122, 2].

Active constituent: Saponins and glycosides [62].

IMAGES

Abrus precatorius Linn.

Acacia arabica (Lam.) Willd.

Acacia concinna (Willd.) DC.

Acorus calamus L.

Achyranthes aspera L.

Aegle marmelos (L.) Corr.

Allium cepa L.

Allium sativum L

Aloe vera (L.) Burm.f

Annona squamosa Linn.

Azadirachta indica A. Juss.

Bacopa monnieri (Linn.) Wettst.

43

Brassica compestris L.

Butea frondosa Roxb.

Calotropis gigantea (L.) Dryand.

Celastrus paniculatus Willd.

Centella asiatica (L.) Urb.

Cicer arietinum L.

Citrus limon (L.) Burm. f.

Clitoria ternatea L.

Cocos nucifera L.

Cyperus scariosus R.Br.

Datura stramonium L.

Eclipta alba (L.) Hassk

Emblica officinalis Gaertn.

Eucalyptus globulus Labill.

Glycerrhiza glabra L.

Hedychium spicatum Sm.

Hibiscus rosa-sinensis L.

Indigofera tinctoria L.

Jasminum officinale L.

Lawsonia inermis L.

Linum usitatsimum L.

Mentha piperita L.

Murraya koenigii (L.) Spreng.

Nardostachys jatamansi (D.Don.) DC.

Prunus dulcis (Mill.) D.A.Webb

Psoralea cordata (Thunb.) Salter

Ricinus communis L.

Rosa damscena Mill.

Rubia cordifolia L.

Sapindus trifoliatus L.

Sesamum indicum L

Tagetus erecta L.

Terminalia belarica (Gaertn.) Roxb.

Terminalia chebula Retz.

Trigonella foenum -graecum Linn.

Withania somnifera (L.) Dunal

Ziziphus mauritiana Lamk.

Zingiber officinale Roscoe.

SUMMERY

In the present study 50 plant species belonging to 47 genera and 35 angiospermic families are listed. Utilization pattern of species indicated flower, leaf, seed, fruit, seed coat, stem, root, rhizome, whole plant etc. Those studied plants are used in various hair problems in India such as hair fall, hair splitting, dandruff, frizzing, dryness, premature hair greying, baldness and lice. It is also used to for maintenance of hair i.e., hair cleaning, conditioning, hair shine and strengthening, thickening, cooling effect, hair tonic etc. Some plants useful for color the hair, to cool the scalp.

BIBLIOGRAPHY

1. Adhirajan A.N., Ravi Kumar T., Shanmugasundaram N. & Babu M. (2003). In vivo and in vitro evaluation of hair growth potential of *Hibiscus rosa-sinensis* Linn. J Ethnopharmacol, 88 (23), 235–239.

2. Ali H. S. & Kadhim R. B. (2011). Formulation and evaluation of herbal shampoo from *Ziziphus spina* leaves extract. IJRAP, 2 (6).

3. Ali E. A. S, (2016). Pharmacological importance of *Clitoria ternatea* – A review. IOSR Journal of Pharmacy, 6 (3), 68–83.

4. Asuntha G., Prasannaraju Y. & Prasad KVSRG.

(2010). Effect of Ethanol Extract of *Indigofera tinctoria* Linn (Fabaceae) on lithium / Pilocarpine-Induced Status Epilepticus and Oxidative Stress in Wistar Rats". Tropical Journal of Pharmaceutical Research. 9 (2), 149–156.

5. Ayurvedic Pharmacopoeia of India. (1999).Govt. of India, Ministry of Health and Welfare, New Delhi. 3:129.

6. Azar H.M., Thikah A.M., & Qubas. N.h. (2009). Treatment of *Alopecia areata* With Topical Garlic Extract. Kufa Med. Journal. 12(1).

7. Back P. (1987). The Illustrated Herbal. Hamlyn Publishers through Octopus Books printed in Hong Kong by Mandarin.

8. Badi K. A. & Khan S. A. (2014). Formulation, Evaluation and Comparison of The Herbal Shampoo With The Commercial Shampoos, Journal Of Basic And Applied Sciences. 301–305.

9. Bahare et al., (2018). *Tagetes spp.* Essential Oils and Other Extracts: Chemical Characterization and Biological Activity, Molecules, 23, 2847, 1-35.

10. Bara K. J., Soni R., Jaiswal S., Saksena P., (2016). Phytochemical study of the plant *Withania somnifera* against various diseases. Journal of Agriculture and Veterinary Science. 9, 109–112.

11. Barnes J., Anderson L. A. & Phillington J. D. (2002). Herbal Medicines: A guide for healthcare professionals Edition. Pharmaceutical Press, London.

12. Barve K. & Digho A. (2016). The Chemistry and Applications of Sustainable Natural Hair Products. Springer Brief Green Chemistry for Sustainability.

13. Basch E., Ulbricht C., Kuo G., Szapary P. & Smith M. (2004). Therapeutic applications of fenugreek. Alt Med Rev, 8 (1), 20–7.

14. Beroual K., Halmi S., Maameri Z., Benlaksira

B.S., Agabou A., Chibat M. & Hamdi Pacha Y. (2014). Pharmacological Aspect Of *Linum usitatissimum*: Flax Ingestion On Hair Growth In Rabbits, J. Nat. Prod. Plant Resour. (4) 1, 4-7.

15. Bhawna K., Kumar S. S., Lalit S., Sharmistha M. & Tanuja S. (2013). *Cyperus scariosus*: A Potential Medicinal Herb, Int. Res. J. Pharm, 4(6),17–12.

16. Biswasroy P., Panda S., Das D., Kar D. M. & Ghosh G. (2020). Pharmacological investigation of *Calotropis gigantea*: A benevolent herb of Nature. Research J. Pharm. and Tech, 13 (1), 461–467.

17. Boskabady M. H., Shafei M. N., Saberi Z. & Amini S. (2011). Pharmacological Effects of *Rosa damascena*.Iran J Basic Med Sci, 14 (4).

18. Chintha V. R., Gandham S., Wudayagiri R. (2018). Traditional, Ethnomedical, and Pharmacological uses of *Celastrus paniculatus*: Review, Asian Journal of Pharmaceutics 12 (4),

1119.

19. Chopra R. N., Nayar S. L. & Chopra I. C. (1956). Suppliment to Glossery of Indian Medicinal Plants, New Delhi: CSIR.

20. Colloredo G., Bertone V., Peci P., Locatelli A., Brembilla G., & Angeli G. (1987). Pseudoaldosteronism caused by licorice. Review of the literature and description of 4 clinical cases. Minerva Med., 78 (2), 93–101.

21. Cooke T. (1903). The flora of the presidency of Bombay. Taylor and Francis, London.

22. CTFA: Cosmetic Ingredient Handbook. 1988, published the CTFA Inc. Library of Congress Catalogue card No. 88-071506.

23. Dahanukar S. A., Kulkarni R. A. & Rege N. N. (2000). Pharmacology of medicinal plants and natural products. Indian J. Pharmacol, 32, 81–118.

24. Dasaroju S. & Gottumukkala K. M. (2014). Current Trends in the Research of *Emblica officinalis* (Amla): A Pharmacological

Perspective. Int. J. Pharm. Sci. Rev. Res, 24 (2), 150–159.

25. Datta K., Singh A.T., Mukherjee A., Bhat B., Ramesh B. & Burman A.C., (2009). *Eclipta alba* extract with potential for hair growth promoting activity. J. Ethnopharmacol, 124 , 450–456.

26. Deb Roy S., Karmakar P., Dash S., Chakraborty J. & Das B.(2014). Hair Growth Stimulating Effect And Phytochemical Evaluation Of Hydro-Alcoholic Extract Of *Glycyrrhiza glabra,* Global J Res. Med. Plants & Indigen. Med. 3(2), 40–47.

27. Desam N., Reddya A., Jabbar A., Sharma M., Mylabathula M., MosesG., Reddy R. &Mohammed A.(2019). Chemical Constituents, *In Vitro* Antibacterial And Antifungal Activity of *Mentha* × *Piperita* L. (peppermint) Essential Oils. Journal of King Saud University Science, 31(4), 528-533.

28. Dev I., Guha S. R. D., Jain K. D. & Swaleh M. (1979). Chemical Study of Sapindus mukrissi

Seed Kemel. Ind. J. For., 2(4), 381-82.

29. Devi Priya M. & Siril E. A. (2014). Traditional and Modern Use of Indian Madder (*Rubia cordifolia* L.): An Overview. Int. J. Pharm. Sci. Rev. Res, 25 (1), 154–164.

30. Dweck A. C., Article for "Cosmetics & Toiletries Indian Plants", Published by Peter Black Medicare Ltd., 1-21.

31. Dweck A. C. (1996). On the *Centella asicatica* trail. Soap, Perfumery and 58Cosmetics Asia. 1, 41–42.

32. Dweck A. C. Article for Cosmetics & Toiletries Magazine Ethnobotanical Plants from Africa Part Two. 1-18.

33. Foster S. & Duke J.A. (1990). A Field Guide to Medicinal Plants and Herbs of Eastern and Central Medicinal Plants, Peterson Field Guides. Houghton Mifflin.

34. Garg V., Kaur B., Singh S. K. & Kumar B. (2016). *Terminalia Chebula*: Success From

Botany To Allopathic And Ayurvedic Pharmacy, Asian J Pharm Clin Res, 9(5), 21-28.

35. Gediya S. K., Mistry R. B., Patel U. K., Blessy M. & Jain H. N. (2011). Herbal Plants: Used As A Cosmetics. J. Nat. Prod. Plant Resour, 1 (1), 24–32.

36. Gopala Krishna A. G., Gaurav R., Bhatnagar A., Prasanth Kumar P. K. & Chandrashekar P. (2010). Coconut Oil: Chemistry, Production and Its Applications. A Review, Indian Coconut Journal, 15–27.

37. Gottumukkala V. R., Mukhopadhyay T., Ranganathan S., Madhavi M. S. L., Annamalai T. & Lavakumar S. (2013). Chemical examination of three Indian medicinal plants and their hair growth evaluation studies Arch. Appl. Sci. Res.5 (5), 126-130

38. Grabley S. & Thiericke R. (1999). Bioactive agents from natural sources: trends in discovery and application. Adv. Biochem. Eng. Biotechnol.64, 101–154.

39. Gupta A. K., Sharma M. & Tandon N. (2005). Quality standards of Indian Medicinal Plants, Indian Council of Medicinal Research, New-Delhi, 2, 132.

40. Gupta A., Malviya R., Singh T. P. & Sharma P. K. (2010). Indian Medicinal Plants Used in Hair Care Cosmetics: A Short Review. PHCOG, 2 (10), 361–36.

41. Heukelbach J., Oliveira F. A. & Speare R. (2006). A New Shampoo Based On Neem (*Azadirachta indica*) Is Highly Effective Against Head Lice In Vitro. Parasitol Res, 99 (4), 353–356.

42. Hooker, Joseph Dalton, Sir, 1817-1911. Flora of British India (1875). Reeve, London, L.

43. Ikram M. & Husssain S. (1978). Compendium of medicinal Plants, Pakistan Council of Scientific and Industrial Research, Peshawar, 1-167.

44. Ilanchezhian R., Joseph R. C. & Rabinarayan A. (2012). Urushiol induced Contact Dermatitis

caused during Shodhana (Purificatory Measures) of Bhallataka (*Semecarpus*. Linn.) Fruit' AYU. 33. 270–273.

45. Ivancheva S., Nikolova M. & Tsvetkova R. (2006). Pharmacological activities and biologically active compounds of Bulgarian medicinal plants. In: F. Inperato (Éd.). Phytochemisry: Advances in research. 87–103.

46. Jadeja B. A., Odera N. K. & Gajera M. R. (2006). Plants Used in Traditional Phytotherapy for Hair Care in Gujarat, India. Scientific Publication, Jodhpur, 258–68.

47. Jahan N., Mushir A. & Ahmed A. (2016). A review on Phytochemical and biological properties of *Calotropis gigantea* (Linn) R.Br. Discovery Phytomedicine, 3 (3), 15–21.

48. Jain R., Kachhwaha S. & S.L K. (2012). Phytochemistry, pharmacology, and biotechnology of *Withania somnifera* and *Withania coagulans*: A review. Journal of Medicinal Plants Research. 6, 5388–5399.

49. Jain A., Dubey S., Gupta A., Kannojia P. & Tomar V. (2010). Potential of Herbs As Cosmaceuticals, 1, 71–77.

50. Jokar A., Masoomi F., Sadeghpour O., Nassiri-Toosi M. & Hamedi S. (2016). Potential therapeutic applications for *Terminalia chebula* in Iranian traditional medicine. Med, 36 (2), 250–254.

51. Kapoor V. P. (2005). Herbal Cosmectics For Skin and Hair Care. Natural Product Radiance, 4 (4), 306–314.

52. Kaur S.& Jaggi R. (2010). Antinociceptive activity of chronic administration of different extracts of *Terminalia bellerica* Roxb. and *Terminalia chebula* Retz. Fruits. Indian J. Exp. Biol. 48, 925–930.

53. Khan I. A. & Khanum A. (2005). Medicinal and Aromatic Plants of India. 1st ed. Ukaaz Publications Hyderabad, India.

54. Khan M. S., Lari Q. H. & Khan M. A. (2015). Physico-Chemical and Pharmacological

Prospective of Roghan-e-Narjeel (Coconut Oil. International Journal of Pharma Sciences and Research (IJPSR, 6, 1268–1272.

55. Khushboo P. S., Jadhav V. M., Kadam V. J. & Sathe N. S. (2010). *Psoralea corylifolia* Linn. - "Kushtanashini". Pharmacogn Rev, 4 (7), 69– 76.

56. Kirtikar K. P. & Basu B. D. (1995). Indian Medicinal Plants. Edn, 2.

57. Khastgir H. N. & Senguptaupta S. K. (1958). The Sapogenin From Seeds of *Achyranthes aspera* Linn. Journal of the Indian Chemical Society, 35, 529–530.

58. Kumar N. & Khurana S. M. P. (2018). Phytochemistry and medicinal potential of the *Terminalia bellirica* Roxb. Bahera), Indian Journal of Natural Products and Resources, 9 (2), 97–107.

59. Lee H. S., Jung S. H., & Yun B. S. (2007). Isolation of chebulic acid from *Terminalia chebula* Retz. and its antioxidant effect in

isolated rat hepatocytes. Arch Toxicol, 81 (3), 211–218.

60. Leung A.Y. & Foster S. (1996). Encyclopedia of Common Natural Ingredients Used In Food, Drugs and Cosmetics. 2nd. edition. John Wiley.

61. Manniche L. (1989). An ancient Egyptian Herbal. British Museum Publications.

62. Mahran G. E., Glombitza K. W., Mirhom Y. W., Hartmann R. & Michel C. G. (1996). Novel Saponins from *Ziziphus spina-christi* Growing In Egypt. Planta Medica, 62 (20).

63. Manosroi J., Jantrawut P., Manosroi W., Kongtawelert P. &Manosroi A. (2015). 5α-Reductase Inhibition and Melanogenesis Activity of Sesamin from Sesame Seeds for Hair Cosmetics. Chiang Mai J. Sci, 42 (3).

64. Marshall J. M. (1990). *Aloe vera* Gel - What Is The Evidence? Pharmaceutical Journal, 360–362.

65. Marwat et al. (2017). *Ricinus Communis*: Ethnomedicinal Uses and Pharmacological

Activities. Pak. J. Pharm. Sci, 30 (5), 1815–1827.

66. Mishra L .C., Singh B. B. & Dagenais S. (2000) Scientific Basis for the Therapeutic Use of *Withania somnifera* (Ashwagandha. A Review, Alternative Medicine Review, 5 (4), 334–344.

67. Mishra T. N., Singh R. S., Pandey H. S., Prasad C. & Singh B. P. (1993). Antifungal Essential Oil and Long Chain Alcohol from *Achyranthes aspera*. Phytochemistry, 31, 1811–1812.

68. Mitaliya, K. D., Bhatt D. C., Patel N. K. & Dodia S. K. (2003). Herbal Remedies Used For Hair Disorders by Tribals And Rural Folk In Gujarat. Indian J. Trad. Knowl. 2, 389–392.

69. Mukhopadhyay G., Kundu S., Sarkar A., Sarkar P., Sengupta R., & Kumar C. (2018). A review on physicochemical & pharmacological activity of *Eclipta alba*, The Pharma Innovation Journal 2018; 7(9): 78-83.

70. Mushtaq A., Mir A. & Muhammad Z. (2008). Traditional Herbal Cosmetics Used By Local Women Communities In District Attock Of Northern Pakistan, Indian Journal of Traditional Knowledge Vol. 7(3), 421-424

71. Naik V. N. (1998). Flora of Marathwada. Amurt Prakashan, Aurangabad Volume I & II.

72. Namiki M., Ahmad M., Khan M. A. & Zafar M. (2007). Nutraceutical functions of sesame, Crit. Rev. Food. Sci. Nutr, 47 (3), 651–673.

73. Nerali S. B., Chakravarti K. K. & Paknikar S. K. (1970). Terpenoids, Rotendene and Rotendenol, Sesquiterpenes From *Cyperus Scariosus*. Ind J Chem. 8, 854–55.

74. Nosal O. G, Mokry J. & Hasan K. M. (2003). Antitussive activity of the fruit extract *of Emblica officinalis* Gaertn. Euphorbiaceae), Phytomedicine, 10, 583–9.

75. Oh J. Y., Park M. A. & Kim Y. C. (2014). Peppermint Oil Promotes Hair Growth without Toxic Signs. Toxicol Res, 30 (4), 297–304.

76. Packianathan N. & Karumbayaram S. (2010). Formulation and Evaluation of Herbal Hair Dye: An Ecofriendly Process. J. Pharm. Sci. & Res, 2 (10), 648–656.

77. Parle M. & Bhoria M. (2010). Almond: A Health, Annals ff Pharmacy And Pharmaceutical Sciences. 1(2), 147–151.

78. Patkar A.N., Desai N. V., Ranage A. A. & Kalekar K. S. (2012). A Review on *Aegle Marmelos*. A Potential Medicinal Tree. IRJP,3 (8), 1–6.

79. Phondke G.P., (1992). The Wealth of India an Encyclopedia of India's Raw Material Resources. Council of Scientific and Industrial Research, New Delhi.

80. Pieroni et al. (2004). Survey on The Natural Ingredients Used In Folk Cosmetics, Cosmeceuticals And Remedies For Healing Skin Diseases In The Inland Marches, Central-Eastern Italy, Journal of Ethnopharmacology. 91, 331–344.

81. Piva, G. S., Weschenfelder, T. A., Franceschi, E., Cansian, R. L., Paroul, N., & Steffens, C. (2018). Linseed (*Linum usitatissimum*) Oil Extraction Using Different Solvents. Food technology and biotechnology, 56(3), 366–372. https://doi.org/10.17113/ftb.56.03.18.5318

82. Prasetiyo A. (2017). Anny Victor Purba, Effectiveness Test Combination Ethanol Extracts of Fenugreek Seed (*Trigonella foenum-graecum* L.) and Cayenne Fruit (*Capsicum annuu*m L. Hair Growth ActivityIjppr.Human. 10 (4), 210–221.

83. Quispe C., Villalobos M., Borquez J., Simirgiotis M., (2018). Chemical Composition and Antioxidant Activity Of *Aloe vera* From The Pica Oasis (Tarapaca, Chile) By UHPLC-Q/Orbitrap/MS/MS, Journal of Chemistry.

84. Ramaiah C. V., Kumar G. S. & Wudayagiri R. (2018). Traditional, Ethnomedical and Pharmacological uses of *Celastrus paniculatus*. Review, Asian Journal of Pharmaceutics, 12

(4).

85. Rao G. V., Annamalai, T., & Mukhopadhyay, T. (2011). Phytochemical Investigation And Hair Growth Studies On The Rhizomes of *Nardostachys jatamansi* DC. Pharmacognosy magazine, 7(26), 146–150.

86. Rao G. V., Mukhopadhyay T., Madhavi M. S. L. & Lavakumar S. (2011). Chemical Examination and Hair Growth studies on the Rhizomes of *Hedychium spicatum* Buch. -ham. Pharmacognosy Communications. 1, 90–93.

87. Rao B. N. S., Rajshekhar D. &. Raju D. C. (1996). Folklore Remedies For Dandruff From Tirumala Hills of Andhra Pradesh. 1, 296 –300.

88. Rastogi R. P., Mehrotra B. N. (1998). Compendium of Indian Medicinal Plants. Central Drug Research Institute, Lucknow and National Institute of Science Communication and Information Resources, New Delhi, 1–6.

89. Rathi V., Rathi J. C., Patel A. & SengodanT. (2017). Hair growth activity of *Cicer arietinum*

Linn. Ocimum sanctum Linn and Cyperus rotundus Linn in Albino Rats. Journal of Pharmacognosy and Phytochemistry, 6 (1), 157–159.

90. Rauf A., Uddin G., Ali J. (2014). Phytochemical Analysis and Radical Scavenging Profile of Juices of *Citrus sinensis, Citrus anrantifolia*, And *Citrus limonum.* Organic and Medicinal Chemistry Letters, 4 (1), 5.

91. Reddy Y. A., Chalamaiah M., Ramesh B., Balaji G. & Indira P. (2014). The ameliorating activity of ginger (*Zingiber oficinale*) extracts against lead-induced renal toxicity in male rats. Journal of Food Science and Technology, 51 (5), 908–914.

92. Roshan S., Sharma P., Gupta R. & Sharma S. *Butea monosperma* A Traditional Medicinal Plant: An Overview. https://www.pharmatutor.org/articles/butea-monosperma -traditional-medicinal-plant-overview

93. Roy G. (1985). Natural Beauty - the practical guide to Wildflower cosmetics. Webb and Bower.

94. Roy R. K., Thakur M. & Dixit V. K. (2008). Hair growth promoting activity of *Eclipta Alba* in male albino rats. Arch Dermatol Res.300, 357–64.

95. Sabharwal S., Sudan S. & Ranjan V. (2013). *Jasminum Sambac* Linn (Motia. A Review, IJPRBS, 2 (5), 108–130.

96. Sachs M., Von Eichel J. & Asskali F. (2002). Wound management with coconut oil in Indonesian folk medicine. Chirurg, 73, 387–92.

97. Sampath Kumar K. P., Debjit B., Chiranjib, Biswajit & Tiwari P. (2010). Allium cepa: A traditional medicinal herb and its health benefits. J. Chem. Pharm. Res, 2 (1), 283–291.

98. Sandeep & Parakh P. (2009). Jasminum grandiflorum Linn (Chameli): Ethnobotany. Phytochemistry and Pharmacology – A review. Pharmacologyonline. 2, 586-90.

99. Sandhya S., Chandrasekhar J., David B. & Vinod K. R, (2012). Potentiality of Hair Growth Promoting Activity of Aqueous Extract Of *Abrus precatorius* Linn. on Wistar Albino Rats. Journal of Natural Remedies, 12 (1), 1-11.

100. Sanwal S. K., Rai N., Singh J. & Buragohain J. (2010). Antioxidant phytochemicals and gingerol content in diploid and tetraploid clones of ginger (*Zingiber oficinale* Roscoe. Scientia Horticulturae, 124 (2), 280–285.

101. Saraswathi M. N., Karthikeyan M., Rajasekar S. & Gopal V. (2012). *Indigofera tinctoria* Linn A Phytopharmacological Review, International Journal of Research in Pharmaceutical and Biomedical Sciences, 3 (1).

102. Shachi S., Jagdamba S. & Shiv K. (2010). New Terpenoid From The Rhizomes of *Cyperus scariosus.* Int. J Chem, 1 (1), 25–30.

103. Shah G. M. & Khan M. A. (2006). Common Medicinal Folk Recipes of Siran. Ethnobotanical Leaflets, Valley, Mansehra,

Pakistan. 10, 49–62.

104. Shah N. C. (2012). Cosmeceutical and Ethno-cosmetics in India. Herbal Tech Industry, 15–20.

105. Sharma P. C., Yelane M. B. & Dennis T. J. (2001). Database on Medicinal Plants used in Ayurveda. In: Central Council for Research in Ayurveda and Siddha. 1–3.

106. Shibu Narayan Jana Sm. C. (2018). Health Benefits and Medicinal Potency of *Withania somnifera.*A Review, Int. J. Pharm. Sci. Rev. Res, 48 (1), 22–29.

107. Singh S. & Singh A. Navneet, Srivastava V. (2018). Ethnobotanical and Pharmacological Benefits of *Achyranthes aspera* Linn.: An overview. Int. J. Pharm. Sci. Rev. Res, 48 (2), 1–7.

108. Soni K. K. & Soni S. (2017). *Eclipta alba* (L.) An Ethnomedicinal Herb Plant, Traditionally Use in Ayurveda. J Hortic, 4, 208.

109. Soni P., Siddiqui A. A., Dwivedi J. & Soni V.

(2012). Pharmacological properties of *Datura stramonium* L. as a potential medicinal tree: An overview. Asian Pac J Trop Biomed, 2 (12), 1002–1008.

110. Srivastava R. K., Singh A., Srivastava G. P., Lehri A., Niranjan A., Ktewari S., Kumar K. & Kumar S. (2014). Chemical Constituents and Biological Activities of Promising Aromatic Plant Nagarmotha (*Cyperus scariosus* R.Br.) A Review, Proc Indian Natn Sci, 80 (3), 525–536.

111. Sudhakar P. & Shashikanth J. (2012). Ethnomedicinal importance of some weeds grown in sugarcane crop fields of Nizamabad District. Andhra Pradesh, India. Life Sciences Leaflets, 10, 51–55.

112. Suneetha J., Rao J. K. & Reddi T.V.V. S. (2011). Herbal Remedies for Hair Disorders by the Tribals of East Godavari District. Andhra Pradesh Journal of Experimental Sciences, 2 (8), 30–32.

113. Suraja R., Rejithaa G., Sunilsona J. A. J.,

Anandarajagopala K. & Promwichita P. (2009). In Vivo Hair Growth Activity of *Prunus dulcis* Seeds In Rats. Biol Med, 1, 34–8.

114. Surjushe, A., Vasani, R. & Saple, D. G. (2008). *Aloe vera*: A Short Review. Indian journal of dermatology, 53(4), 163–166.

115. Tamara et al., (2018). Lemon As A Source Of Functional And Medicinal Ingredient: A Review, IJCBS. 1455-61.

116. Trivedi R.V, Bansod P. G, Taksande J. B, Mahore J. G, Tripurneni S. R, Rai K. R. & Umekar M. J. (2019). Investigation of hair growth promoting ability of herbal gel containing *Zingiber oficinale*. Int. J. Res. Pharm. Sci, 10 (4), 3498–3507.

117. Vibha P. & Singh. N. (2016). Plants Used In Herbal Shampoo. ijipls, 6 (3), 287–293.

118. W.H.O. (1999). Who monograph of Selected Medicinal Plants? Vol-1. World Health Organization, Geneva.

119. Wijaya W. H., Mun'im A. & Djajadisastra J.

(2013). Effectiveness test of fenugreek seed (*Trigonella foenum-graceum* L.) extract hair tonic in hair growth activity. Vol. IJCR. 5(11):3453-60.

120. Xu G. & Xu C. (2000). China Patent CN 98-114250 19980821.

121. Yadav S., Anil Kumar, Dora J. & Ashok Kumar (2013). Review Article Essential Perspectives of *Lawsonia inermis.* International Journal of Pharmaceutical and Chemical Sciences. 2 (2), 888-96.

122. Yoon J.I., Al-Reza S.M. & Kang S.C. (2010). Hair Growth Promoting Effect of *Zizyphus jujube* Essential Oil. Food. Chem. Toxicol, 48, 1350–1354.

123. Younus M. (2015). Ethno Botanical Study and Traditional Uses Of *Celastrus paniculatus*, IJISET. International Journal of Innovative Science, Engineering & Technology. 2, (11).

124. Zadeh J. B. & Kor N. M. (2014). Physiological and pharmaceuticaleffects of

Ginger (*Zingiber oficinale* Roscoe) as a valuable medicinal plant. EuropeanJournal of Experimental Biology. 4, 87–90.

125. Zahid M., Mujahid M., Singh P. K., Farooqui S., Singh K., S P. & Arif M. (2018). *Annona squamosa* (Custard Apple): An Aromatic Medicinal Plant Fruit With Immense Nutraceutical And Therapeutic Potentials.Linn. Int J Pharm Sci Res. 9 (5), 1745–59.

126. https://www.biodiversityofindia.org

127. www.cosmetics.co.in/cosmetic-products.html

128. http://folkmedsindh.com.pk/cicer-arietinum-l/

129. https://indiabiodiversity.org/

130. https://elmaskincare.com/herbs/herbs_butterfl y_pea.htm

131. https://www.indianmedicinalplants.info/herbs/ index.php/sanskrit- names-of-plants

132. https://regrowz.in/key-ingredients/murraya-leaf-benefits

133. https://regrowz.in/?utm_source=regrowz.com

134. http://www.theplantlist.org

135. *www.tropicos.org*

136. https://www.dreamstime.com/free-photos

www.ingramcontent.com/pod-product-compliance
Lightning Source LLC
Chambersburg PA
CBHW041107280526
45792CB00010B/2335